WISD🅞M
STORIES

WISD⊙M STORIES

A collection of short stories & reflections to
help guide you through everyday life

Book 1

Bhaskar Goswami
STORYTELLING & REFLECTIONS

Fruzsina Kuhári
ILLUSTRATIONS

Christine Joy Décary
DESIGN

For more information, please contact
Bhaskar Goswami at bhaskar@globaldaana.org

ISBN 9781707897421 (Paperback)

Illustrations by:
Fruzsina Kuhári
www.DesignFK.com

Book Interior & Cover Design by:
Christine Joy Décary
www.ParallelBranding.com

Also by Bhaskar Goswami

(Available at BhaskarGoswami.com)

Wisdom Stories (Audio) - Wisdom encapsulated in story form. Ancient, modern, global. Humor, insight, suspense. For all genders, ages, cultures. This is ol' school storytelling. No scripts!

Open Yoga (Audio) - Professional yoga practice CD with live music by multiple Grammy nominated Adrian Carr on piano.

Dedications

This book is dedicated to all the lovers, keepers and creators of inspiring stories.

This book is also dedicated to my three beautiful children Jai, Eva and Uma.

May these stories continue to inspire future generations.

Contents

Foreword

So much is lost in translation. Mystics from all cultures and traditions have experienced profound and life changing insights. These insights were passed down for the benefit of future generations through an oral tradition. They went through several cycles of interpretation by their lineage of students, and were eventually transcribed. These transcriptions were then translated into various languages, adding further to the distortion. Finally, due to the shortsightedness of a few, the teachings were sometimes consciously manipulated for personal gain.

So the bearers of wisdom devised another way to preserve the purity of the original insight: **to encapsulate the wisdom in a story**. This way, no matter how much the words may change, the essential insight still remained intact. Otherwise, the story would not work. It would lose all remarkability because stories carry the felt experience. Better yet, everyone loves a good story!

All my favorite teachers are storytellers. Stories have a way of bypassing that part of the brain that is hardwired with unexamined beliefs. It has a disarming quality in that, it's not about me, it's just a story. Then suddenly, the insight hits me with a giant 'Aha!' in a way that would have taken me years to understand with just theory. Also, it is so much more fun and playful! So often, when my life jams up, a story shows up from the archives to help me skillfully navigate through it.

There is a notes section at the end of this book for you to jot down any of your 'Aha!' moments along the way. I hope that you enjoy these stories and that they are of benefit to you, as they have been for me.

With much love,
Bhaskar Goswami

Nasruddin & His Keys

One morning, Nasruddin was outside his house, searching frantically. A friend came by and said, "Hey Nasruddin, what's the matter?"

Nasruddin looked up and said, "My keys! I lost my keys!"

So, out of compassion, the friend also joined the search. They searched and searched through all the leaves, twigs, branches and bushes. Other people saw them searching and they also joined the search. Like this, time went by, one hour, two hours.

Finally, one person stood up and said, "Nasruddin, we've been out here for two hours now. Where did you lose your keys?"

Nasruddin responded, "Oh, I lost my keys inside the house."

Everyone stood up bewildered, "Nasruddin, why

are we searching for your keys outside your house if you lost them inside the house!?"

Nasruddin said, "Well, it is very dark inside my house. Very hard to search in there. It is much easier to search outside."

Reflection

Isn't life like that sometimes? Whenever life gets problematic, there is a tendency to look for the solution outside where we can see so much better. Yet the key might actually be inside this house called 'the body'. But it is very dark in there. The purpose of mindfulness practice is to bring some light into this darkness so that we can find the keys so much more easily.

One way to look at it is, we all enter into life empty-handed, and leave life empty-handed.

All we have in the middle are a series of experiences. A successful life or a happy life, would be a life that has pleasant experiences. All experiences have only ever happened within this house, this body called 'I'. This story is a wonderful invitation to enter into this body, turn the light on and find these precious keys to happiness.

A Farmer's Tale

In a quaint Italian village, there lived an old farmer. One day, the old farmer received a letter saying that he had inherited the horse of an uncle that passed away.

As they often do, that evening all the farmers gathered around a campfire to share their stories. Upon hearing about the farmer's inheritance, all the farmers said, "Hey ol' man, you are so lucky! You got a horse for doing nothing."

The old man said, "Maybe."

A few days later, the horse arrived at the farm. As soon as the cart door opened, the horse raced out, jumped over the fence, and headed off into the woods. That evening, when all the farmers got together, they said, "Hey ol' man, you are so unlucky. You only had the horse for a few moments, and it ran away. So sad!"

The old man said, "Maybe."

Two days later, the horse returned with six other wild horses from the forest. Now the farmer had seven horses! That evening, all the farmers got together, and they said, "Hey ol' man, you are so lucky! You have seven horses!"

The old man said, "Maybe."

The next morning, the farmer's son decided to train and tame the inherited horse. As soon as he got on the horse however, the horse flung him into the air. He fell down hard and broke his leg. That evening, all the farmers got together and said, "Hey ol' man, your son who is so valuable on the farm, has broken his leg. So sad."

The old man said, "Maybe."

It so happened that the country was in a war at that time. The army was going from village to village recruiting all the young healthy men. When they came into the farmer's home, they saw the boy with a broken leg and said, "This boy is useless", and they kept on going. That evening, all the farmers got together and said, "Hey ol' man, you are so lucky. Your son broke his leg at exactly the right time. My son has gone to war. I don't know if I will ever see him again. At least you still have your son. You are so lucky."

The old man said...

"Maybe."

Reflection

As the first century philosopher Epictetus very wisely said, "We are not disturbed by things, but rather, by our opinion of things". Ancient wisdom traditions have also said that people, places, things and situations are empty or void of qualities. It is our opinion that gives them the qualities. In my own life I have experienced so many times, when I felt that I had achieved some success, and around the corner there was a huge fiasco that was waiting. From the huge fiasco and around the next corner, there was a tremendous success that was waiting. Always changing, ebbing and flowing, coming and going.

As the wonderful Sufi poet Rumi said, "Out beyond ideas of wrong-doing and right-doing, there is a field. I'll meet you there". That field, of 'maybe'!

The Samurai Story

S amurai are highly disciplined warriors, with tremendous mastery over their body and their mind. They have a very refined practice.

In a little village in Japan, there lived a samurai master. He had the respect and appreciation of all the villagers, particularly the farmers, because he was protecting them from a tyrannical landlord that was trying to enslave them.

One day, the landlord got very frustrated. He decided to kill the samurai master, and he was successful. He put a bit of poison in the master's tea one night, and the next morning the master passed away. The landlord was so happy! Now that the samurai master was gone, he could have his way with the farmers. What the landlord did not realise was that this master had a disciple, a student, a young warrior who was also very respected by the dojo and by the community. Let's just say, the force was strong in the young samurai warrior as well.

The code of the samurai is 'blood-for-blood'. When the samurai warrior found out that his master was killed by the landlord, from a place of duty, he went after the landlord. When the landlord heard about this, he immediately took flight. And so the chase went on for two years! The samurai warrior chased the landlord all around Japan.

Finally, one fateful day, the landlord was trapped. He ran into a house, and the samurai warrior followed. He ran into a room in the house, and the samurai warrior followed. Now the landlord was totally trapped in the room. He ran to a corner and cowered. The samurai warrior came right up to him and started to remove his sword from its sheath.

Suddenly, the landlord looked up and spat at the young warrior! The warrior looked back down at the landlord, put the sword back in its sheath, and walked out of the house.

This one is really a question story: *Why did the samurai warrior walk out of the house?*

(Take a moment to reflect on this)

If we rewind back two years to when his master was killed, the warrior went after the landlord from a place of duty, reverence and obligation towards his master. Fast forward two years from there to when he felt the saliva landing on his body, he also felt a movement of anger inside his body. To kill the landlord from a place of anger would be a disrespect to his master.

So, he walked out of the house, cooled off, came back and then finished his obligation. Gruesome story! Nevertheless, it points to something very beautiful. The ability to observe emotions rather than reacting to them. It is the difference between 'I am angry' and 'there is anger'. It's a small change in words, yet a big difference in experience.

Reflection

A disciplined mind is able to observe even the inner terrain. As we cultivate mindfulness, the ability to observe our own emotional terrain, we see all these emotions that come, stay for a while and go: fear, anger, excitement, sadness, joy, depression. Skillful living comes from being able to respond to our emotions rather than react to them. One definition of integrity is someone who takes the whole into account. An integer is a whole number. A person with integrity takes everything into account. Not just what is happening externally, but also what is happening inside this mind body structure called 'I'; and responds accordingly.

Put the Woman Down

One day, a senior monk was walking with his disciple from village to village through a forest. Along the way it started to rain quite heavily. They got to a path where they saw a lady who was reluctant to cross the path because it had become very wet and muddy. Without any hesitation, the senior monk scooped up the woman, put her on his shoulder, walked across the path, put her down and kept on walking.

The young disciple that was trailing behind him was shocked. He could not believe it! This is a senior monk, forbidden to have any contact with the opposite gender. He could not believe that his master did that.

Time went on and after a while  the young disciple said, "Master, I have to ask you this question. How could you, a senior monk, lift up a woman like that? You are supposed to have no contact with the opposite gender! How could you do that?"

The senior monk looked back at his young disciple and said, "I put the woman down two hours ago. Why are you still carrying her?"

Reflection

We all have our version of the 'woman on the shoulder' that we are carrying. It could be some memory, some 'to do' list or something that you are looking forward to. Essentially, anything that has absolutely nothing to do with what is happening in the present moment. This story to me is an invitation to put that down, the heavy baggage of past and future, and be more present.

The Golden Buddha

L ong time ago, in a remote village in Vietnam, there happened to be a massive statue of a golden Buddha. It was so magnificent! It was the prized possession of the village.

One day, the news came that their land was being attacked by an invading army that was advancing from village to village. The villagers got very concerned for the statue. Of course, it would be destroyed. Then, one villager had the brilliant idea of covering up the statue with mud. So all the villagers got together, padded up the statue with mud, carved it to look like a perfect mud statue of Buddha and then ran away from the village.

Sure enough, as the army came, they disregarded the mud statue, took what they could and moved on. The village laid bare for several decades. After a while, a whole new settlement came into the village. None of them knew that the statue was actually golden. They lived like this for several years.

Then one day, on a hot afternoon, a young monk was meditating in front of this mud statue. As he opened his eyes, he saw something glistening in the corner of the statue. Being very curious, we went up to the statue and scratched away at it. He was shocked to discover that there was gold under the mud. He immediately ran into the monastery and said, "Gold! The statue is made of gold!"

All the monks came out, removed the mud and restored the statue to its original golden nature.

Reflection

This story reminds me that we are all born with that original 'golden Buddha nature'. This original enlightened, awakened, spontaneous, present state. Then as life rolls along, through fears, perceived or otherwise, we tend to protect or cover up our golden nature with the 'mud' of personality, ideas and beliefs. Eventually, out of either good grace or the sheer heat of experience, the mud starts to crack. We suddenly realise, "Hey, there is actually gold in there! Ah, I forgot about that." Then, just like the monks from the monastery, all the wisdom teachers help us chip away the mud and restore us to our original golden nature.

Chakravartin & Mount Sumeru

The word 'chakra' means 'wheel' and 'vartin' means 'unstoppable'; the unstoppable wheel. Back in ancient times there were rulers of empires. The more civilized way in which they attacked a neighbouring empire was to adorn their best horses with a beautiful golden chariot. They then let the chariot enter into the neighbouring kingdom.

Now, the ruler of the neighbouring kingdom had a decision to make: If he captured the chariot, this would mean that he has started a massive war that could take the lives of thousands and thousands of people. Or, he could just let the chariot wander through his land, which meant that his kingdom was peacefully captured, and the original ruler's kingdom had just expanded. So, a Chakravartin was a ruler whose wheel was never impeded. To put it another way, a Chakravartin is someone who ruled the entire world.

Chakravartins are very, very rare. Even Alexander

the Great, who died young at 32, only captured half the known world. To capture the entire world is a very, very rare feat indeed. This is the story of one such Chakravartin.

Chakravartins are so rare that they get a very special entry into heaven when they die. They enter into heaven with their entire entourage of advisers, soldiers, wives and so on. When this Chakravartin died, he entered into heaven feeling very accomplished, very dignified. He was of course received with a great deal of honor and reverence in heaven.

Chakravartins are given a very rare privilege. In heaven, there is a mountain called Mount Sumeru. Mount Sumeru is the most majestic mountain, ten times the size and grandeur of the Himalayas. It is made entirely of gold! In heaven there are thousands of suns, not just one. So there were thousands of suns shimmering on this magnificent golden Mount Sumeru.

The privilege of being a Chakravartin is that he is able to chisel his name on this mountain. All this time, this Chakravartin's mission and aim was to have his name on the mountain.

He moved towards the glorious mountain with his entourage following, and met up with the mountain keeper. In heaven, people live a very long time, so this mountain keeper was thousands of years old. With respect, he bowed down to the Chakravartin, and handed him a hammer and a chisel. As the Chakravartin was about to enter through the gates, the mountain keeper said, "With much respect and reverence, I suggest that you leave your entourage behind, and go and chisel your name by yourself."

The Chakravartin was shocked at this suggestion! What was the point of going there and chiseling his name by himself? Where was the grandeur and glory in that? It would only be special if his entourage could see this. Yet, he looked at the mountain keeper and saw that there was no malice in him. He did not mean any harm.

The mountain keeper went on to say, "Listen, why don't you go, have a look and if you want to come back and get your entourage, they will be here."

The Chakravartin found this to be quite reasonable, so he went to the mountain. When he got to the mountain, hours upon countless hours went by as he looked all around the mountain for a space for him to chisel his name. On the entire mountain, there was not a single space available for him! The mountain was completely covered in the names of past Chakravartins.

He was so shocked to discover this, and also, so humiliated. All this time he had felt that he was so special, and just then he realized just how unremarkable he actually was. This universe has been around for eons and eons. Thousands of years means nothing. So many Chakravartins have come and gone.

Very embarrassed, he headed back to the mountain keeper and muttered sheepishly, "Oh my goodness, there isn't a single space for me to put my name on the entire mountain!"

The mountain keeper laughed and laughed! He said, "I've been here for thousands of years. This was the job of my father and my grandfather. There has not been a single time when any Chakravartin found any space to engrave their name. I tell you what, why don't you go back to the mountain, erase somebody's name and put your name?"

The Chakravartin looked at him bewildered and said, "What's the point of that? It's just a matter of time before somebody comes along, erases my name and puts their name. *What's the point of that?"*

Reflection

This is a story about ambition. If we just do things for ourselves, "me, I, mine" and keep collecting titles, accolades and possessions, what's the point of that? It's all been done before. If we can do things that somehow uplifts others, makes others feel good and benefits others, this has a way of resonating for generations and generations. This is a true legacy. This is called 'karma yoga', or selfless service. When we keep enough to sustain ourselves and the ones that depend on us in an agreeable way, and the rest is for the good of others.

Two Rings

Once there was a man who was successful by all means and measure. He had all the material pleasures, he lived a purposeful life and was very loved and respected by his community. When he passed away, his two sons moved into his mansion with their respective families.

A few months later, it was not really working out, so the two sons decided to divide everything half-half. They sold the house and went from room to room alloting all the contents. When they entered their father's room, they opened a drawer, and in that drawer they discovered a little pouch. When they opened this up, they found two rings inside.

One of the rings was clearly very valuable, glistening with precious stones and metals. The other one was just an ordinary metal band, a little trinket. The older brother, perhaps a little greedy, said, "This expensive one seems to be a family heirloom. Father did not buy this. Since I am the older son, I should keep the more expensive one and you keep the other one." The younger brother did not argue, and kept the little trinket.

Fast forward thirty years or so, the older son was a complete wreck. He was so mentally and physically worn out and looked so old. The younger son however, looked almost exactly the same as he did thirty years ago. *What happened to make such a huge difference?*

(Take a moment to reflect on this)

We rewind back thirty years and find the younger son walking away from the house, looking at the ring and wondering to himself, "Father wore both these rings. I understand why he wore the more expensive one. It is such an impressive piece of jewelry. But why did he wear this little band?"

As he became curious, he examined the band very carefully. On the inside of the band he noticed the words inscribed, *"This too shall pass".*

"Ooohhh.. This too shall pass! This is what father has been telling us all his life. This too shall pass." The younger son put the ring on his finger as a reminder, *this too shall pass.* So when life was a sweet song, a summer breeze, and everything was going great with health, relationships and career, he enjoyed it. Yet he had the understanding, this will pass. When it was the winter of discontent, everything was going wrong, fiascos, miscommunications, health issues, he took it smilingly. The ring reminded him, this will also pass.

And so all the ebbs and flows, ups and downs of life were skillfully navigated with this profound understanding, this too shall pass, so why get hung up on it? The secret to long lasting youth is the understanding: It is all going to pass, so let's enjoy what is.

Reflection

This story is a reminder of impermanence. Everything that we have ever known in this causal universe, a universe of causes and effects, has always changed. Every experience that I've ever had, every sight, sound, taste, touch, scent, thought, emotion. Every place that I've been to and every person that I've met. Everything had this one quality in common: **impermanence.** Once we really understand the notion of impermanence, experientially, we can move through life in a more light and uplifting way. Good for ourselves, and good for others.

Birbal & the Challenge

B ack in ancient times, kings used to walk around with their wisdom counsel by their side. There was once a very well known king called Akbar and his wisdom counsel was called Birbal.

Early one morning, Akbar the king, decided to take a dip in a passing river. As soon as his body entered the water, it was so freezing cold that he leapt right out and said trembling, "Oh, the water is freezing! I will give any person their weight in gold if they are able to stay in this river for an entire night."

Word soon spread around the kingdom of king Akbar's challenge. A couple of days later, a man came along to accept the challenge. That evening, a crowd gathered by the river, Akbar with his guards and Birbal by his side, watching as the man calmly walked into the river, neck deep. He just stayed there in a perfectly peaceful state. Hours went by and the man did not move.

Come the light of dawn, the man calmly walked out of the river.

Akbar was shocked! He could not believe that the man could stay in the river so calmly for so long. True to his word, he was about to give the man his weight in gold. Then he asked the man in all curiosity, "That is amazing what you did. I wonder, how did you manage to do that?"

The man responded, "Well, do you see that village in the distance over there? In that village there is a hut, and in that hut there is a candle lamp. I just focused all my attention on the candle flame, and it kept me warm all night."

Akbar became very furious. He said, "Well in that case, you cheated! You will not get your weight in gold." The man, disillusioned, walked away, the crowd dispersed and Akbar returned to his palace.

A day or two later, Birbal was missing from the palace. Akbar relied on Birbal for wisdom counseling. So he went to Birbal's home with a couple of his guards to look for him. In the backyard, he found Birbal sitting in front of a small burning fire pit, beside a massive tree. Tied high up on the tree, there was a pot with water in it; a far distance from the flames. Birbal was just waiting.

Akbar asked, "Hey Birbal, what are you doing?"

Birbal said, "Oh, I'm just waiting for the water to boil to make my tea. Once it is ready, I'll come to the palace."

Akbar said, "What nonsense! How is it possible for the water to boil when the fire is so far away from the pot!?"

Birbal looked at Akbar with a wry smile and said, "Well, how is it possible for the man to stay warm when the candle flame was so far away?"

Akbar suddenly realized what a terrible mistake he had made by not living up to his promise. He called the man back, and gave the man his weight in gold.

Reflection

Here is what I really like about this story: Birbal is such a wise man. He could have easily told Akbar the moment the man was denied his due, "This is a wrong thing you are doing. You should give the man his due. He did what he said he would do." Yet, instead of giving the king some kind of theoretical or rational knowledge, Birbal instead chose to give the king an experiential understanding of the absurdity of his decision.

Another thing I like about this story is the power of cultivating attention. What a remarkable thing that the man could focus so intensely on one tiny candle flame so, so far away. So thoroughly, that he became that flame. This is a very powerful example of **where attention goes, energy flows.**

The Three Thieves

One day, a wealthy man was walking through a forest when he got attacked by three thieves.

One thief said, "Let's beat him up and take all his money!" They did that.

The second thief said, "Let's tie him to a tree and leave him to rot." They did that, and they went away.

Later in the evening, the third thief came back, untied the man, and showed him the way home.

Reflection

This simple story is about the three qualities in all that is experienced. In the ancient yogic texts they are called Rajas, Tamas and Sattva; the three Gunas, qualities of Maya, which is the Cosmic Illusion. The first one, Rajas, is very belligerent, hyperactive and violent. The second one, Tamas, is very dull, inert and atrophying. The third one, Sattva, is very pure, peaceful and wholesome.

All that we know has one of these three characteristics. For example, certain foods tend to overstimulate, certain foods tend to make us dull, and certain foods are light and nourishing. There are certain people who are prone to being hyperexcited or nervous, others who are prone to dullness and fatigue, and some who are calm and vibrant. Likewise, certain practices have a hostile and aggressive quality, certain practices have a very dull and lethargic quality, and certain practices have a very healthy and uplifting quality like nature walking, yoga and meditation.

They are all considered thieves in that they rob us of the truth and keep us in the illusion. Yet the last thief, the sattvic thief, unties the bondage created by the first two and shows us our way home to our original self.

The Bear Trap Story

One day a man was walking through a forest and he noticed a mechanical contraption on the ground. He recognized it as a bear trap. Fear arose inside him. He wondered, "What if there are bears in this forest?"

As the man walked along and turned the corner, there was a massive grizzly bear a short distance away. Fear heightened in the man, "What if the bear comes towards me?"

Story being story, the bear ran towards the man. Very heightened fear, "What if the bear grabs me!?"

The bear grabbed the man. Even more fear, "What if the bear attacks me!?"

The bear attacked the man's arm. Still more fear, "What if...!?"

Reflection

This story beautifully illustrates that fear and all its hues like anxiety, phobia, neurosis and stress, are all in the 'what if'. They are all a projection into the future. One simple way out of fear is to shift from 'what if' to 'what is'. It may be that, if the man was in the state of 'what is', in a pure present state, he would be more relaxed. We know that animals can sense fear so the bear might have left him alone. Or the man might have cued into an escape route. Because his mind was so stunned and captured by 'what if', all that 'is', was lost.

Similarly, anger, depression, resentment are all caused when the mind is stuck in 'what was'. So the way out of suffering 'what was' and 'what if' is to come into that razor's edge of 'what is'.

The breath is a wonderful anchor into the here and now.

The King & His Beggar Son

Once there ruled a very wise and respected king. He wanted to make sure that his son, the sole heir to the throne, would also rule wisely. He had a very strange way of accomplishing this.

When his son was of a young age, the king told his son, "You can forget about being a prince. You are now cast away from the kingdom." They took away all of his princely possessions, dressed him in rags and sent him away from the kingdom.

So it was, years and years had gone by. The beggar-prince was now a young man. One day, under the hot afternoon sun, he was begging outside a luxury hotel. There were many people walking by, absolutely indifferent to his condition. He was looking for some coins to buy himself some used shoes to protect his feet from the sheer heat of the burning sun.

Suddenly, a majestic chariot pulled up beside the

beggar. It caught the attention of all the passers by. Out walked a nobleman towards the beggar, and said, "Your father, the king, is now an old man and he said that you are now ready to rule the kingdom."

Immediately, all the people who were so indifferent to him, started to celebrate and they all wanted to become his friend. The beggar boy instantly changed into a prince. It was a very stark and sudden change. He stood tall and said, "Well, take me to the palace so that I can get my hair and body cleaned, wear my new princely clothes and present myself as a prince to my father."

That evening, when the young man was with his father, he said, "Father, why did you do that?! Why did you cast me away when I was so young? I had almost forgotten that I'm a prince. Any longer, I would have died a beggar."

The king said, "Son, I know you must be angry with me, as I was with my father when he did that to me. It is important for you to see both ends of the spectrum, from the beggar to the king and all the people that exist in the middle. It is important for you to see that all these things are external, they can be given and taken away. May that nurture in you the wisdom to rule this kingdom well."

And so he did.

Reflection

This story is a wonderful reminder of how descriptions, titles and labels come and go. It is a parable that teaches us to serve with utmost sincerity and without being so easily distracted by awards and accolades.

Crazy / Genius

One day, a man was driving along and suddenly his rear tire blew out. He stuttered to a halt in front of this massive building that happened to be a mental asylum. The man stepped out of the car and used a jack to lift up his car. He removed the lug bolts and took out the flat tire. Just then, he accidentally knocked the four lug bolts into the drain. He became so frustrated!

"Now I am stuck! What am I supposed to do?!" he grumbled to himself as he stood there scratching his head.

It so happened that a man from the mental asylum building was looking outside his window and he witnessed the whole thing. He shouted down, "Mister! Mister!"

The man with the flat tire looked up and said, "Yes?"

The man from the window said, "Sir, why don't you take one lug bolt out of each of the other tires? This way you will have three lug bolts in every tire. Good enough for you to get to the mechanic and get the car fixed properly."

The man with the car stood in stunned silence and finally said, "My goodness, that is brilliant! What are you doing in a mental asylum?"

The man from the window responded, "Sir, I may be crazy, but I'm not stupid."

Reflection

I love this story because it points to the understanding that although genius and stupid might be dimetrically opposite, there may be a very thin line between genius and crazy. This story reminds me to pay extra attention when something appears to be crazy or genius. I may have them mixed up! I joke that the difference between crazy and genius is profit. If it makes a profit, it is genius! If it doesn't, it's crazy.

The Truth

One dark night, a massive naval battalion ship was patrolling the ocean. In the distance, they saw a light shimmering back. The captain of the battalion ship signalled using Morse code, "Please change your direction. We are heading directly towards you."

A few moments later, he received the response, "We will not do that."

The captain became frustrated and he said, "We are a naval battalion ship heading directly towards you. Change your course now."

A few moments later, the response came, "I am sorry, we will not do that."

Now the captain became absolutely furious! "This is the SS Eisenhower, the second biggest naval ship in the entire US navy. If you do not change your course immediately, we will be forced to bombard right through you!"

A little while later, the response came, "Sir, we are a lighthouse."

Reflection

No matter how intense life may get, the truth is like a beacon that shines through, steady and unmovable. This story is an invitation to remember that, no matter the situation, the truth does not compromise.

Thorn in Foot

One day, a man was walking through a forest on his way home. Along the way, a thorn broke in his foot and made his journey very uncomfortable. So, the man bent down, removed a thorn from another twig and used that thorn to remove the thorn in his foot. Then, he threw both the thorns away and comfortably walked home.

Reflection

All these stories, as wonderful as they are, are not the experience of wisdom. They are also thorns. Yet, they are useful thorns to remove old thorns of beliefs, ideas and opinions that might be making our journey through life uncomfortable.

We throw all the thorns away and return home to our original wisdom.

Stay Connected!
Join the Wisdom Stories Tribe

Wisdom Stories - Book 1 is the first of a series of books. To learn more about future releases and to connect with a like-minded tribe of Wisdom Stories readers, please make sure to join us on social media. You will find us on Instagram and Facebook.

@WisdomStoriesTribe

Use **#WisdomStories** so we can find each other, share our experience of these uplifting stories and enjoy any 'Aha!' moments together. We would love to know how these stories are helping bring joy and clarity for you.

Find out more at **WisdomStories.ca**

See you soon in the online community!

About the Author

 Bhaskar Goswami is an acclaimed speaker and a senior yoga and meditation teacher from Assam, India. He has led numerous international retreats and has presented in prestigious organizations and events like **COP22** (UN Global Climate Change Summit, Morocco). In 2007, he founded **BODHI**, a multiple award-winning company dedicated to offering genuine wellbeing to people in their homes and workplaces. He is also the founder of **daana** (CBC Media Prize 2016, Startup of the Year), a non-profit organization making wellness accessible to all by creating anonymous contribution-based uplifting activities around the world. He has published two international albums, **Open Yoga** and **Wisdom Stories**.

Bhaskar has a Masters Honors in Electronic Engineering from the University of Nottingham (England) and a 10-year international engineering career. He lives in Montreal with his family of three children.

Learn more:
BhaskarGoswami.com

About daana

daana means 'cultivating generosity' in Sanskrit. This is the foundation of all religions and cultures. In ancient times, wisdom teachers taught generously, and the students appreciated the teachings in the spirit of generosity. Princes gave jewelry, businesspeople gave money, farmers gave food and those with little means prepared the food or cleaned the place.

daana is also a non-profit organization that is retelling this simple and profound story in a modern context. **daana** offers an opportunity to cultivate generosity towards ourselves, towards each other and towards our global community for generations to follow. This is done by making anonymous contribution based 'gift-it-forward' uplifting activities accessible to all. It is a story about co-creating a world on the foundations of wellness, community and generosity. If this has inspired you in any way, you are already a part of it!

To discover more, please visit:

globaldaana.org

Notes

Notes

Notes

Made in the USA
Middletown, DE
12 August 2024

58491152R00061